Intimations

by
Caroline Urvater

All rights reserved. Except for brief passages quoted in newspaper, magazine, radio or television reviews, no part of this book may be reproduced in any form or by any means, electronic or mechanical, including photocopying or recording, or by an information storage and retrieval system, without permission in writing from the author.

Professionals and amateurs are hereby warned that this material, being fully protected under the Copyright Laws of the United States of America and all other countries of the Berne and Universal Copyright Conventions, is subject to a royalty. All rights including, but not limited to, professional, amateur, recording, motion picture, recitation, lecturing, public reading, radio and television broadcasting, and the rights of translation into foreign languages are expressly reserved.

ISBN 978-0-692-03317-3
Caroline Urvater © 2016

Typesetting and cover design by Yu Chien Liu

Intimations

by
Caroline Urvater

For Madelina

Table of Contents

Rhymes
- Ode to an Egg ... 10
- Socks ... 11
- Dieting ... 12
- Visiting D.C. ... 13
- Spring ... 14
- So What ... 15
- Aging ... 15
- Central Park in Spring ... 16
- Lines to an Absent Therapist ... 17
- The Fat Cat ... 18

Poems
- My Need ... 22
- Spätlese ... 23
- Transplants ... 24
- Endings ... 25
- Misery ... 26
- Nothing ... 27
- Friendship ... 28
- Doors ... 29
- To E.M.U. ... 30
- I Am Sorry ... 31
- Dreams ... 33
- Journeys ... 34
- Weddings ... 36
- Maine Wind ... 37
- Fog ... 38
- Darkness ... 39
- French Squares ... 40
- November ... 41
- Last Resort ... 42
- Summer ... 43
- My Poems ... 44
- The Letter P ... 45

Rhymes

Ode to an Egg

O egg, I perceive in your ovular roundness
The basic requirements for structural soundness.
I salute you, combining aesthetic appeals
With elementary essentials for nourishing meals.
How sweetly it nestles, your yolk in its bed,
With what dainty precision your albumen's spread.
For me your fine nature is ever unsoiled,
Fried, scrambled or poached ~ nay even hardboiled.
The saints all be praise for the great moment when
You popped forth in your glory from out of the hen,
But sometimes I wonder, as all cynics do,
Did you pop from the hen, or'd the hen pop from you?

Socks

Most pairs of socks inhabit drawers
And cover feet adjacent.
This constant closeness often bores
Or makes them feel complacent.
Sometimes the most devoted sock
Will suddenly quit its mate,
And disappear without a trace,
Leaving its spouse disconsolate.
Somewhere inside the washing machine
Deep, deep within an unseen crack
A host of straying, single socks
Lies hidden, never to come back.
The abandoned mate does not last long,
Cast off, rejected by its owner.
Only the absent sock survives
And in some secret spot it thrives,
Obscure, unseen, a loner.

Dieting

Each morning as I wake I say:
"I'll start my diet now, today."
And as I drink my morning tea
I say: "I'm doing this for me."
Then sometimes even lunch is brief
As I feed on a lettuce leaf.
But comes the ebbing of the day
My resolution fades away.
By eight p.m., I admit defeat
And eat and eat and eat and eat.
Then late at night when I repent
And wonder where my will power went,
I promise in the throes of sorrow
That I will try again ~ tomorrow.

Visiting D.C.

I sit on a marble bench in Washington D.C.,
Watching the passing populace in the home of the brave
   and the free.
Yet after half an hour or so I'm sorry that I have come,
There's nothing like a marble bench
For making your rear end numb.

Spring

In this old husk new life abides
As in the bulb a crocus hides.
When winter, banished, yields to spring
The cold earth thaws, then new birds sing.
And overhead where white clouds play
Warm winds will blow cold winds away!

So What

So what if you are old and fat
And bald, and everything like that?
For I myself am past my prime
And have been so for quite some time.
I love you, dear in spite of all I see,
Largely because of what you used to be.

Aging

As I grow older I am torn between despair and hope
Concerning the disparities with which I'm forced to
    cope.
I am not appalled at aging, but what is such a shame
Is that my outside's getting older while my insides stay
    the same.
People I meet can only see my wrinkled, aging hide.
So few perceive the lively soul that lives in me ~ inside.

Central Park in Spring

Central Park's benches fill as soon as there is sun.
Old gentlemen in natty suits watch children as they run.
On other benches grandmothers with burnished hair
Sit elegantly and enjoy the warming air.
Brown nursemaids rock small kids in Italian togs,
And everywhere one sees all sorts of dogs.
Their owners so resemble them that one forgets
Which are the owners, which the pets.
A pigeon puffs his feathers, fans his tail.
The female busy pecking crumbs, ignores the male.
Later, she squats. The ritual has begun.
He pops on top of her, and then they're done.

Lines to an Absent Therapist

There's no one who knows what I'm thinking
For my shrink is out of town.
Who cares if my spirits are shrinking
'Cause my shrink is out of town.
My date book is blank Monday morning
While my shrink is out of town.
My bank account grew without warning
Since my shrink went out of town.
I'm forgetting my troubles with no one to tell
While my shrink is out of town.
He better come soon or I'm going to get well
While my shrink is out of town.

The Fat Cat

My mother abandoned me when I was born
So I sat on the sidewalk all starved and forlorn.
One day as I lay half-dead on the street
I was found by a couple who thought I looked sweet.
Then I left the city for New Rochelle
Which was something like going to heaven from hell.
At first, I was happy just to roam through the house,
There was plenty to eat there, although never a mouse.
But as I got older and grew sharper claws
The sweet time were over THEY laid down the laws.
No sharpening on furniture, couches or floors,
No sitting on armchairs, no going outdoors.
I could look out and see the world, but not smell it or
  taste it.
What good is a squirrel unless you have chased it?
I could see the birds strutting, right there in plain
  view.
They laughed as I watched them. Not a thing could I
  do.
When spring came a stirring arose deep inside me.
The she cat next-door-but- one finally spied me.
She drove me insane as she walked through my yard
With her tail in the air. Oh. It really was hard
Not to claw my way out through the mesh of the
  screen
And do things to her that were rather obscene.
So I sprayed on the windows and scratched all the
  walls

And shattered the night with my anguished cat calls.
The result of my nocturnal vocalization
Was a trip to the vet for the dread operation.
I returned to my home with a real sore behind,
A new disposition and no sex on my mind.
But life seemed so empty, I really felt beaten
Except for those moment when I had just eaten.
Food was my focus from that moment on.
Eating became living, my blues were soon gone.
The years go by sweetly and swiftly at that
And I'm known far and wide as that very fat cat.
I sit in the kitchen where the food is located
And stuff myself hourly until I feel sated.
I let people pet me sometimes when I'm bored,
But if they annoy me they always get clawed.
I have very little use for the whole human race,
They don't seem to know how to keep to their place.
My owners are well trained; they obey me okay,
Though they are too dumb to understand much that I say.
So I sit at the window or I sleep in a chair.
I spend time on my toilet by grooming my hair.
Time passes easily; life is so sweet
As I gorge myself till I feel really replete.

Poems

My Need

This is my need when everything fails me:
The wind, the sea, the comforting curve
Of a Chinese vase
In the Metropolitan Museum.
This is my need when the child of my heart
Hurts me, or my lover deserts me.
I need to return to the earth which I came from,
To the gentle heave of the sea,
To the howling surf.
From the folds of the cliffs
I can see the horizon
The cloud strewn sky
The rock strewn shore.
Here, I feel one with the wind and the waves,
Here I need nothing less, nothing more.

Spätlese

These days I take my tea alone, by choice.
My hormones having given up their voice,
I live my single status and rejoice.
Oh, I have known much of deceiving,
Of passionate couplings and of leaving.
Now, with my children grown my life is mine,
And I am free to make and follow my design.
This is not to say that sometimes I don't sigh
When twining lovers catch my watchful eye.
The pang, however, swiftly passes by!

Transplants

Pass on my useful parts if I should die.
One is myopic, but I do have one good eye.
My kidneys work. I've always found their action
Efficient, and entirely to my satisfaction.
My liver, too, has served without a hitch,
Complaining only when my diet gets too rich.
But don't expect to save my heart. It was abused
So badly that it cannot be reused.

ENDINGS

Endings are difficult
They are
Letting go
Leaving
Stopping
Wrapping up
Releasing
They also mean
Freeing.
Over means above, but also ended

Finished is ambiguous
It also means completed
Done is cooked and over
Stopping is ending
Perhaps silence is best.
It is no sound
Unsound.

Misery

It is so easy to write a poem
When you are happy, loving.
But when your "we" dissolves
And your eyes are red in their salty baths
Then there is nothing to celebrate
And misery doesn't rhyme with anything.
It is a feeling so pain-filled that it is unbearable,
Yet you bear it because what else can you do?
Where can you go when there is nowhere you want to
　go,
When a chance word locks your throat because it was
　someone's favorite?
O the terrible, lonely, grayness of being alone, un-
　loved, unloving.
Color recedes and your very breath stabs you.

Nothing

Nothing consumes itself and grows.
A storm replenishes.
Hail bruises, lightening scars.
The wind uproots,
But nothing vacuums life.
The sun burns, heals.
Snow covers and seals.
Nothing defeats my anger
and my hope and pain.
Not rage, but silence kills.

Friendship

There are several kinds of friends.
There are the proximity friends: neighbors, co-workers,
People with whom you feel an affection that dissipates
When you are no longer near one another.
Then there is the friendship, often the love
One feels for a teacher during the intimacy of
  studying together.
A student experiences a passion for a great teacher
and erroneously feels that this passion is reciprocated.
  It is not.
Some friendships endure for decades. They are few
  and rare.
They are affected neither by distance nor by silence,
  nor by the passing of time.
These friendships are planted in the heart. Sometimes
  they become dormant.
But they can always be revived. When they bloom
  again
These relationships continues where they left off.
There are friends that one loves, and others one
  dislikes,
But they cling like gum.
Friendship is an amalgam of affinity, longevity and
  reciprocity.
When people meet and feel an affinity for one
  another,
They must be prepared to wait.
No friendship is instantaneous. It is like dough that
  must be mixed,
Given time to rise and then slowly baked until it
  becomes an actual loaf.

Doors

A door closes. Exclusion. A smile dies.
Waiting every night, fists clenched under my quilt,
for my door to open and close.
A looming shape in the half-darkness
touches me, panting.

A sunny morning. No sound where there should have
　　been one.
In an act of cowardice for which I can never forgive
　　myself,
I send my husband. Horrible silence.
There will never be another sound.
I am no longer a mother.

Morning light on a stairwell, breakfast sounds through
　　an open door
as I descend I hear: "Oh no not again."
The door closes.

To E.M.U.

Every time you leave
A membrane is slowly torn
From my heart.
I feel as though I have touched a block of ice,
And my flesh has stuck to it.
While I pick off the thousand strands
That have grown, twisted around us,
I feel pangs as shiveringly deep
As the pleasures we once enjoyed.
When I look at you
I see an anxious boy peering through
Your middle-aged face.
He seems to be asking if the punishment is over
So that, at long last, he may go out to play.

I AM SORRY

I am sorry, most of all because our year together
Was an extraordinary, passionate, multicolored, all absorbing
Year of closeness, of newness of sweet, long nights, deep talks
And the delighted, repeated discovery of affinities.
It was soft flesh, lines and curves, and crinkly hair surrounding a tonsure.
The wildness and exhilaration of it was thrilling, yet
I sensed that those great heights would soon give way to their opposite.
That was my year. Not yours.
Oh yes, for a while you were fascinated, but that too
Soon gave way to something I wasn't part of.
Something I didn't see.
My year was exquisite. It took my breath away.
You panicked. You couldn't endure.
You slid helplessly away from me, back to your peripatetic solitude.
I went down into a colorless, sleepless void that slowly filled with tears.
Now I am coming back. Gradations of light surround me.
Music flows into me. I am regaining myself.

Dreams

Stout is a wonderful word.
It evokes my aunt Margot.
She was tall with white wavy hair
A commanding nose and
A voice that was worn and creaky.
She complained that her daughter
(who was also stout, tall with grey hair,
But had inherited her father's insignificant nose.
However, she did have beautiful grey eyes)
wouldn't listen to her dreams.
Margot said "I have reached a time in life
In which my dreams have more substance and reality
Than my days do."

Now *my* dreams are tangled and jumbled
I must express them out loud so that I can decipher
their meanings.
Now I have reached that state where
My dreams are messages I have sent myself.
They are wrapped in mysterious forms
They heave and undulate, peopled with familiar faces
That speak to me soundlessly.
In my dreams I am always young and often invisible.
I reach out trying to touch those people,
They ignore me.
Suddenly someone takes my elbow
And pulls me away from the others.

I wake up with a jolt, with the strands of the undeciphered
    dream
Festooned over me. I try vainly to go back to sleep
Then I lie in a tangle of sheets
Trying to understand what I was telling myself
And I remember Margot.

Journeys

I used to take trees for granted until I saw
the last, stunted oak in western Kansas
trying to suck sustenance from the gritty land.
I had never known that there was not much sky in New
 York
until I saw Colorado. On the plains there is nothing
but a huge sky and the distant Rockies,
sharp in the ungenerous air.
I rode a horse in Wyoming. All day I rode
under a vast metallic blueness. The land was flat.
Silver-grey plants clung to the flinty ground.
I saw an eagle and a shimmering herd of antelope.
They were all I saw all day in that blazing, rainless
 land.
I was an alien there. My skin darkened and dried;
my hair hung straight; my nails became brittle.
When I closed them, the insides of my eyelids
 scratched my eyes.
So I fled back to the moist, dark east.
Here, the sullen sky hangs like a soiled sheet waiting
 to be washed.
Here, weather sneaks in scudding clouds behind
 skyscrapers.
Skyscrapers make their own weather in their windy
 canyons.
Beneath the city there is another, skyless city.
Rain drips through gratings from the upper world.
Bright rails herald the approach of the train.
Twin ribbons of light unroll themselves along the rails

as the clattering train bears down on the station.
In that grimy-tiled world there are Orfeos playing.
Here the homeless lie in their itchy, restless sleep.
Inside the trains the air is rank with a thousand sighs.

I am at home. I was born in sleety rain and fogs
under lowering skies in the loamy smell of decaying
    logs
where, teeming marshes squelched under foot.
Now I find the footprints I made long ago.
I find the rock on which I lay.
It held my body as though I were cradled by God.
There is no god, but, there is still the rock.

I am on my way from somewhere to somewhere,
a lonely journey yet not one I make alone.
I have finished traveling from place to place.
it is time for the interior voyage.
The one best made without baggage.
I have joined the ranks of the faceless, milkless
    mothers,
Of the husbandless wives. The sad ranks that trudge
    away from the sunrise.
That turn their backs upon summer.
Yet autumn is all around us, long and glorious.
Decay has a rich smell of ripeness and closure.
The immense afternoon moves slowly to twilight.
As the shadows grow longer and slant towards
    evening
I lie on my rock and wait.

Weddings

Watching other people's weddings saddens me. I remember mine.
At the first one I was afraid that daddy, that dark eminence,
Would suddenly materialize at the critical moment to forbid it.
The second time I married, in what I thought was my full maturity,
After I had two children with number one,
After I had lived three years with number two. I feared no one.
My father was dead and I knew what I was doing. Or so I thought.
But I forgot to notice that my new husband had betrayed my predecessor.
In my arrogance I believed that this time he would be different.
It took me years to see what others knew and saw.

So I am fearful at other people's weddings. I feel like the old crone
Who comes to the christening and curses the baby.
Cassandra-like I look into the dazzled young faces;
Closing myself against the insistent palpitation of the music, of the heartbeat beneath the sounds.
It is terrifying to contemplate repetitions!

Maine Wind

This city wind that swings the neon signs
And drives the crumpled rubbish on the ground,
That chills us to the bone and peevish whines
Shaking the window shades with hollow sound.
This midnight wind that hurls the sleety rain
And whistles, icy drafts across the floor
Is not the wind in Southwest Harbor Maine
It goads the grey Atlantic to a roar.
Like a blind giant blundering on the rocks
That wind bends trees and snaps the tauter pines.
It shakes the harbor walls with shocks
Of icy waves and frothing, freezing seas
Then turning inland, whirling blizzard flakes,
It piles up drifts; makes mountains with its blast,
Smashes the ferns, solidifies the lakes,
Then rushes northward when winter's past.

Fog

When the sun blazes so that every leaf
Reflects its sharp, green rays,
And the lake glitters and smashes
The light into millions of flashes,
When the sky is a shattering blue,
I long for fog.

Darkness

If you go out through the kitchen door
closing it quickly so small, white moths
that crave the light, won't come inside
to swirl around lamps like warm snowstorms.
Then once outside, darkness cloaks you.
The sky takes on a black pearl's glow,
And the slow moving lake
Is turgid and dark as a lava flow.
Looking back, you see the light from your
   room compressed in the window.
It is an orange glow like a squared off sun.

FRENCH SQUARES

How I detest those sad French squares
Where plane trees stand with all their limbs lopped off
Like Thalidomide children
Gravel coats the ground with small sharp shards.
Everything in me cries against those grassless places
And their cold, grey, earthless spaces.

November

In cold November as I walk fingered by icy winds,
I feel barren and lone like a leafless tree.
Gone is the summer; gone the warm air
That rose from the earth in a pine scented breath.
The lake's silken waters have turned to ice.
The ferns have shriveled. The moss is dead.
Now city walls rise, flinty and chill,
Imprisoning me.

Last Resort

My home is in my head
where I can hide in many rooms.
My windows are my eyes. I see,
But who sees me?
I move from place to place
Watching and gauging
Until I find the spot where it is safe for me to stop
And close my eyes to dream that I am home.

SUMMER

Summer was cold this year.
I spent my days evading memories,
Stumbling unaided along familiar paths.
I saw the Northern Lights and turned my back.
I left the blueberries to rot
And bought a box from Oregon.
I slept alone.
Slowly I took my island back and had myself as company.
One day I heard a song and found I was the singer.

My Poems

My Poems are not crafted,
They surge out of me like long held breaths.

Your love inhabits me.
It is a painful pleasure,
A disconcerting interruption.

When all the fruit has fallen from the tree,
The tree still reaches upward
But its roots claw downward into earthy depths.

I, inside my aging skin, feel an electric yearning
For the whole of you; your mind, your body.
This is my final surge it shudders in me
So that I do not dread its end.

The Letter P

My autistic granddaughter, whom I love more than anyone else,
Writes lists of names and words beginning with the same letter.
  When I ask her why she does this she looks at me mutely.
I want to enter her world. I want to understand who she is.
So I am doing the same as she does to see how it feels.
I choose the letter P.
I am thinking of pigeons and professors.
New York pigeons just stand there.
The males are always on the make, puffing their neck
  feathers,
Cooing, fanning their tail feathers, turning round and round
Desperate to mate.
They aren't afraid of people who walk by,
But they run from children, cars, hawks and dogs.
They are flying bags of shit.
When a pigeon craps on you people say it is good luck.
What else could they say?
Professor are something else.
The best of them are powerful sorcerers.
Great teachers are charismatic. They uncover treasures.
The best among them are beguiling, not necessarily good
  people,
But hypnotic.
My purest love goes to professors. I am not distracted by their
  bodies.
I worship their minds.
I am no closer than ever to entering Madelina's world. She
  remains,
Kind, beautiful and remote.

Second Avenue

Second Avenue

Collins Homestead MDI

Maine Pond

Backyard Colorado

Inside my mind

Who Am I?

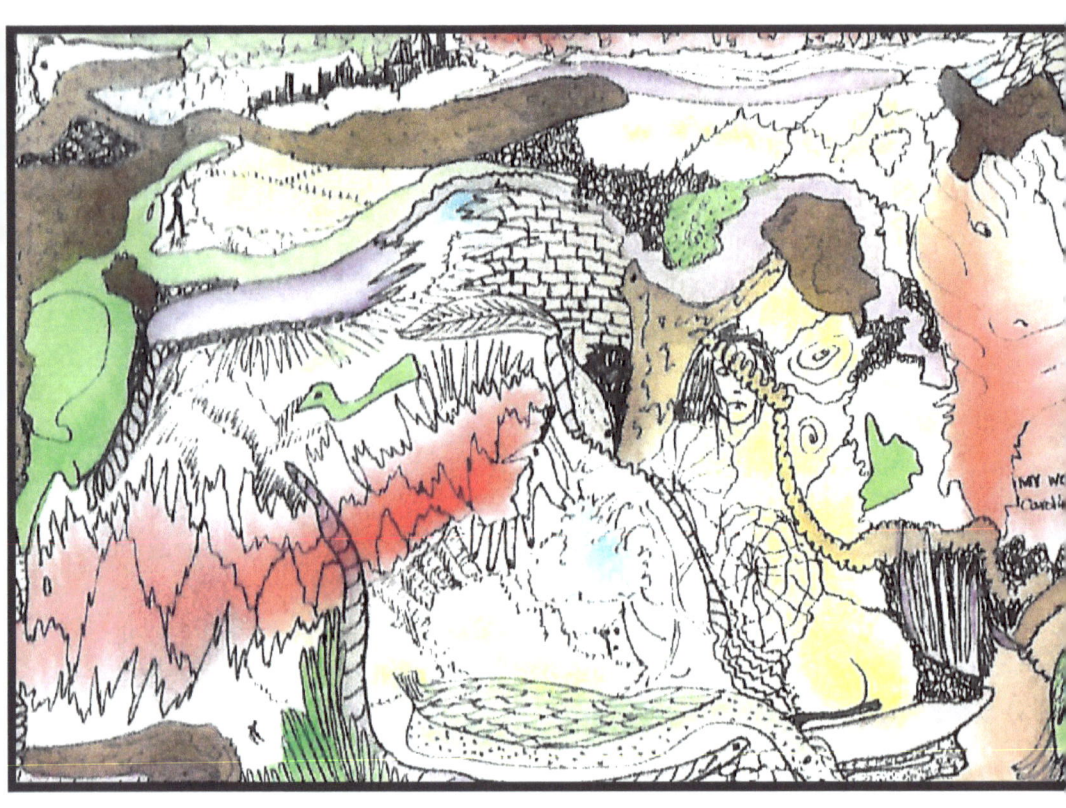

My World

Harry Eating his Children

Uschi Dog

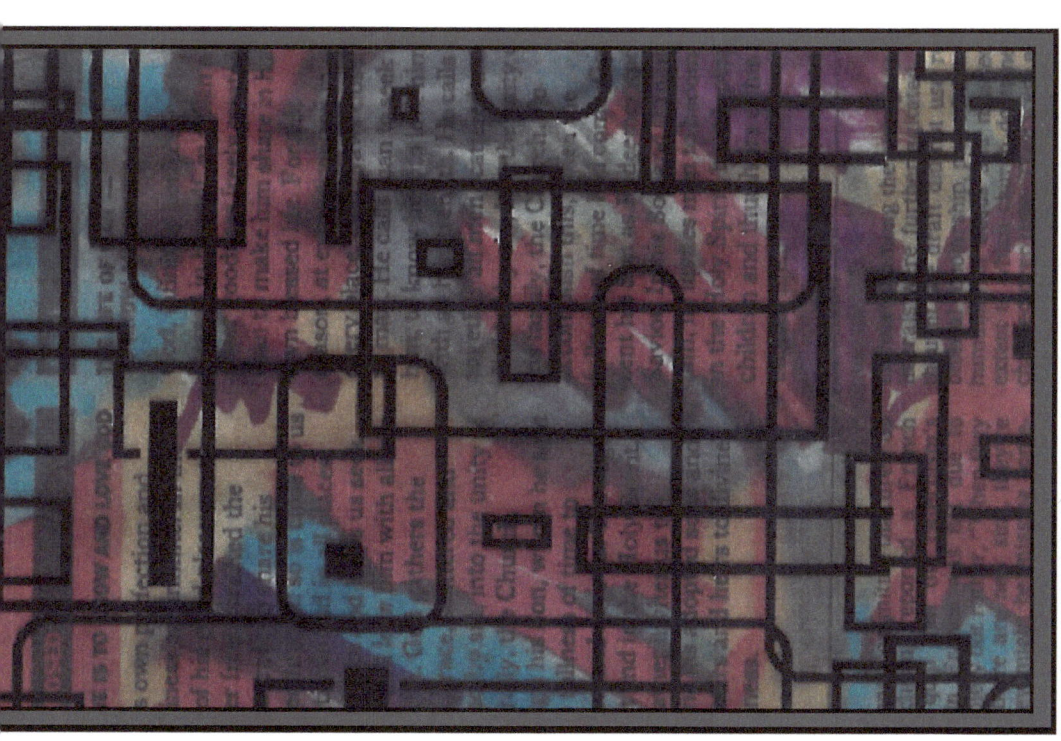

Transparency